# Goodbye Again

## by

## Ron Whittle

Much of this book was written in a time in my life before the Vietnam war. Some of the prose was written at that time, most have been written as thoughts and recollections of a time when living was confusing. Life comes at you fast and hard. Just as you think you have it figured out, it starts the downhill slide towards eternity. The poetry is in random order with no particular direction much like my life has been. I do wish to thank all those involved in my life that have influenced my writing. Especially to Kathi Keddy Giotta, for whom none of this would have seen the light of day. Thank you one and all.

Ron Whittle

To contact the Author, send Email to whittle_ron@yahoo.com

Published by Human Error Publishing
Paul Richmond
www.humanerrorpublishing.com
paul@humanerrorpublishing.com

ISBN:
978-0-9973472-9-6

# Table of Contents

# One last trip to the ocean before winter sets in

Somewhere between here and there
and a mile or so beyond nowhere
who can be sure about such things
yet somehow it was close to the sea
Undulating dunes rose up to meet the sky
on this heavily traveled Cape Cod road
on the other side lay large asphalt meadows
neatly striped out for individual parking
awash with blowing and drifting sand
We walked a path that was roughly the truth
with red stained dune control fencing on either side
hoping to protect the National SeaShore
Facing the breeze it was salty and somewhat warm
as the dune grass swayed back and forth
A short distance from the meadow
we could hear the surf
relentlessly pounding the shoreline
It was all under bright blue skies
with cotton white clouds
We walked downward on a gentle slope
and the sea popped up from behind
the vegetation and beach plum bushes
It was all that I had remembered
but summer was long over before
we had finished enjoying it
There would be no swimming today
just sitting in the sand
and watching the surf and the occasional gull fly by
It was much too cold for summertime fun
but our pre winter day trip was worth it
to preserve our thoughts of the summer solstice
before the snow geese fly south

# Never offered Never found

The truth never lies, it only forgets
and will whisper my secrets
and all of my what ifs
My truth may not be
the same perception as yours
It's all a matter of believing in
what you want to
I left with less for having given more
or did I take what was given as I needed it
I don't know anymore
Perhaps, it only matters
when lovers meet
not where the road bends
but if they see it through
when it turns to gravel
The soft rain weeps
on my empty arms
every now and again
and the soil is all wrong
where roses refuse to thrive
I have become so damned accustomed
to people accepting certain parts of me
and rejecting the others
The aftermath of you
and a man with two useless hands
holding nothing but memories

# It's another 8 beer night before the morning after

Whether we want to be or not
we are bound together
as part of life experiences
All I ever wanted to say
was how much I loved you
If I know you like I think I do
you carried a rainbow into the future
I on the other hand carried a rifle
and a broken heart
Who am I to tell you
who you should be
When I have trouble showing the world
who and what I am
Sometimes I get strangled
in my own sentences
and I don't know if I mean them
I can never look in a mirror again
it's someone else's reflection
not mine
I'm not the old man
staring back at me
In the end all I fought for
was for naught
any bravery that might have been
was left there
on a meaningless piece of ground
I bled on
I needed you like the air
I breathed
I couldn't leave you there
with my blood
I had already left you once
I thought I had survived
I was wrong

## Knowing where her edges begin and end

You may think these kisses
are a clever distraction and disguise
for a Poet
to have another reason
to write about you
In all honesty I want to
fight over a fairytale
that doesn't exist
then go make one of our own
All I want to do is destroy you
in the most beautiful way
I know how
and who says
there is something wrong
with a woman with a naughty side
I mean I could totally
go for some of you right now
this very second
and I really and truly believe
your clothes would look good
on our bedroom floor
Besides I want to see
you with my own eyes
and learn where you begin
and I end

# In black and white only

My memory is in black and white only
Technicolor is for my dreams
My door is no more than a port of entry
into the black and white
and on further entry color explodes into view
In dreams I kiss the sweet wine from your lips
There is a depth to me you have never known
It took me years to find it
and even longer to cultivate it
and why is it so hard for you to believe
that there is so much more to me than you think
Is nighttime really a black and white memory
and how deep is the blue of the technicolor sky
in the dreams I dream
I want to reach back to when I was twenty-two
young and brash unafraid of the world
I had already been through the hell of war
and should have been looking for peace in my life
instead too frightened of the reality
of the here and now
I was too busy refusing to show it
and trying to find a place where I would fit in
and finding no acceptance for me or my brothers
I want to go back to that time and cry when I couldn't
and expose my weakness to the world
I was not the person I pretended to be
and like many others of that time I suffered in silence
There is a whole decade I do not remember
vanished with the black and white memory
that no one will understand except those
that have forgotten too

# The shadow

The weight of your shadow
carries heavy on my back
I took that from you
I took the life from your shadow
No one else knows it is there
but I do
you have no use for it anymore
your body is dead and gone
and your shadow
carries heavy on my back
and weighs heavy on my mind
I see it in my dreams
and it's never far from me
no more than an arm's reach
just so I don't forget
and it forces me to remember
what I have done
and what the call to war can do

# Graffiti

The truth lies in the graffiti
painted on the sides of freight trains
those semi holy words
masturbate the thoughts in my mind
and the excitement builds
as the freight cars pass
I read them as I would read a book
of poetic rhyme
each freight car is like turning a page
and I wait for the final stroke
of the painter's brush
to learn in detail of the uncertain future
of mankind

# The Sea

If ever anything happens to me
cremate me and have my ashes scattered
into the sea
The sea is a good listener you know
we've talked before
The sea will know what to do with me
and every time you go to the shore
know that, I am with you in some small part
in the sand on the beach
the rush of a wave
or the crashing surf
I will be there
forever

come talk to me

# Answering for the sins of yesterday

The war is
branded on my skin
and etched in my mind
Fresh are the smells
of sweat and blood
My ears still ring
from daily gun fire
The burns on my hands
and arms
from ejected shell casings
are a constant reminder
of the lives I have taken
and I can never be
who I used to be
I can only be
what I have become

# Empty frames

I have empty frames
hung in my gallery
with only an idea
for paintings
not yet created
Dry paint brushes
in jars sit by the easel
on the workbench
with the paints and charcoals
I can't bring myself
to put paint to canvas
when my words and thoughts
are in the way
Once I painted us
on a torn canvas
which seemed appropriate
at the time
and tragedy painted itself
with picturesque scenes
of pastel flowers and tears
I thought I threw it all away
along with every word
I never told you
about my undressed desires
and how much
I loved you

# Leaving is a war you don't come back from

My demons come and go
I never know when they will
come back
I know enough not to feed them
but to deny them is a bigger mistake
and there are things about tomorrow
we cannot know about
nor can we change
there are things that no one tells us about
I had to learn on my own
I had to learn the hard way
So many burned bridges
that I must rebuild
and I'm not as strong as I used to be
I need to make everything right
starting with
The whispered I love yous
that you never heard
knowing full well, they are
well beyond their expiration date

# Vietnam

You are the one
that starts the war
I am the bullet
that starts the battle
I am the emptied shell casings
left out on the battlefield
You are the blood
That runs deep into the ground
I am the one
who has to live
with what I have done
I am the one
that carries the lifetime burden
and you are the one
with eternal sleep

# Photographs don't always tell the truth

Sometimes my heart
tells me to walk
somewhere else
I don't always listen
and regret it later
stepping over the
bricks and broken glass
the memories
behind me
there is nothing left
to hold onto
We were much
too beautiful
for photographs

# That was then

Somehow the stars know your name
and the wind begins to sing it
If I showed you my soul
in all its nakedness
would I scare you away
I'm more fragile than you think
and I'm afraid to show it
that was then and now is here
Regret is a feeling
I don't like to call up
but I do so every night
I remember the first time
I saw you walking towards me
I knew I would spend the rest of my life
with you one way or another
and here I am
not that way
but another

# We were young once

I am almost certain there
has been no improvement
in my temperament
It's hard to come back from
being someone you didn't want to be
in a place you wanted no part of
War came rushing at us
as high school graduates
we did what we had to do
and saw what we didn't want to see
Too new to life to fully understand
and too early to have it snuffed out
Fear played its hand
and was immediately trumped
by survival instinct
Some had no choice
it was made for them from
the business end
of a barrel of a gun
triggered and sighted by the enemy
With absolute certainty
I can say life has been interfered with
and has forever been altered
changed in ways
some will never understand
Unseen wounds
that break and tear at the spirit
and heart of a young man
The solace he could not find
anywhere he looked
and there is no privacy in bleeding
or leaking life on the field of combat
Survival depends
on the willingness to live
and the determination
to never give into the call of death
when it dials up your number

The phone is ringing

Don't answer it

# The first time all over again

Love is always a dangerous
game of hide and seek
I buried myself in your sugary sweets
Lovingly imprisoned in your grasp
The touching of hearts
quivering from your kiss
This is where the battlefield begins
I would have fought to the death of me
but you never fought back
The dangers here are fraught
with both right and wrong
Wrong prevailed
When all I wanted was to hear
you say "don't go"
My fear was an enemy
you could not conquer I guess

I would have given anything
to kiss you like it was
the first time all over again

# The crime of passion

How long must one perform penitence
for the love he has thrown away
before he can get off of his knees
and be forgiven for his crime of passion
I was bulletproof in those days
or at least I thought I was
until the tears shot holes right through me
and changed everything

# And to love me is even worse

Why is it the people
who try the hardest to do the right thing
always appear to be mad
And why is it I am the thesis
of thought and pain and equally as mad
Shattered within the broken glass
of the closed window of my dreams
I see things in the reflections
as they should have been
but it's much too late because
love doesn't love anybody and
doesn't care who it hurts
and there within the ruins
and shards of broken glass
lays a broken heart
on a printed bloodied sheet of paper
that reads
Be sure to read all instructions
before attempting to love this device

# Listening 1969

The sun came up this morning
it found me face up in the sand
hands behind my head
listening      just listening
to the sounds of the sea
waves breaking
gulls squawking
the occasional beach walkers
indistinguishable muffled talk

My eyes are closed with visions of you
Lying here beside me
Smiling like you always do
I'm so afraid to open my eyes
for fear that you won't really be here
The sun lights up your face
your eyes are hidden behind dark sunglasses
the wind gently plays with your hair
you smell like suntan lotion
and taste just like the beach
this is how I remember you
on a hot summer morning so many years ago

If I had ten minutes to go back in time
I'd go back to that beach
to that very moment
and tell you how much I love you
and how lonely my future is going to be
without you

# The son of hunger

There is a pleasure of my pen in hand
and writing the words from my heart to mind
The sawdust that raised me
runs deep in my veins
and the common sense my father taught me
protects me
I do not build anymore
but, I repurpose my dreams
and stare at the sky

There is no war in the clouds
and when it comes to the rain
it is like liquid meditation for my mind
But in the distance I can't help but hear the rumble
and see the dark clouds on the horizon
I want to fly
and be whisked away from here
to be there where you are
Away from this secret war
and today is not the day
I wish to touch heaven

My soul reaches out
into the unknown
where my feet touch the ground
and in that moment it stops raining
and just for a second, I had a vision of you
I needed to cry
but found I could not
So instead I bled with it
The last kiss of no hope at all
Disregarding the obvious danger
in the position I am in
hidden behind dark trees
almost naked and nearly invisible
I take careful aim

Death is a lonely man

afraid of everyone
but perfectly willing to kill to stay alive
and finding I am the man,  that the boy does not know
nor understand
but one he will have to live with
along with his secrets, revolting and so very dark

# Somewhere in the woods

I didn't keep my promise
But, I did keep my word
We all have eyes and we don't always see
We all have ears and we don't always listen
We all have hearts and we don't always feel
It's always been a matter of choice
and somewhere in the woods
a tree dies leaf by lonely leaf
and we the servants to the ungrateful lords
load the cannons
fan the flames and feed the fires
and claim what we believe is rightfully ours
Why is it the weapons of politics
enslave us in it's poverty
and pain walks barefoot to the fruitless dead tree

somewhere in the woods

# It has no bearing on what it is

How come
it's never there
it's always everywhere
I never put it

# In the footprints I leave behind

My tapestry of emotions weave their way
with multiples of different types of knots
Each knot represents a type of emotion
and I have lived, lost, and lusted
but found through life's experiences that
love shows no mercy
for those so inclined to fall
Who do I thank for my falling in love
When love knows no bounds
and doesn't answer questions
and does not have feelings
but will hold onto the memories
and pain of love's loss forever
How do we smile at each other
when dying is so easy and living so hard
Who really wants to know the truth I ask
When the truth is so painful and brutally honest
and it wasn't until
I figured out, it wasn't who I loved
but why I loved
did I finally feel free of my social burdens
and it's truly only the lonely
that can answer love's desperate questions

# The portrait of the wolves' lair in two parts

Part one

The wolves of war were hungry in those days
The pieces of me lost to the war
wish to be forgotten
but I still have visions of talking to your picture
as though you were standing in front of me
Confessing that it felt so right
when my lips touched yours
and how bad it felt knowing it never would happen again
I guess when it comes down to it
the words are just empty air expelled from my lungs

Like the light distorted
through the smudged glass windows of my mind

Part Two

The wolves howled at the light of the moon
and sensed the smell of blood and death
that was provided by the war
I stand with gun in one hand and pen in the other
and I paint a picture of colorless words
in the moments leading up to
the bloodletting
The alumni of this and other such events like it
are survivors like myself
that still fight the fight
and wait, much like I do

for my lips to meet hers, once again

# It's only me

What was
was
What is
is
I cannot bring
back what was
What is
is what I live in
and neither
will ever meet

# In and out of tune

Okay this is how the story goes
I should have picked up the pieces
and put them in your hands
I'm not sure why I didn't
Pardon me while I breathe the life out of me
I burned out before I was able to restart the fire
and it's true sometimes we mourn the living
as much as the recently departed

I try not to limit my words in these situations
and it's always been my fear that someone else
could burn a candle brighter than mine
There was a time, tho I can't remember exactly when
I wanted to put my head on your chest
just to count the number of heartbeats you loved me with

I didn't want you to be a part of the effect smoke
and disappear somewhere into the night
and there was no magic wand to wave
or spell that I could have used
that could have ever saved you from me
I always knew I was in and out of tune
and didn't know the last stanza of our song
but that doesn't mean I didn't love you
It only means I didn't know how to tell you

# In the town of Angels

Once upon a time
we were both Angels
I was yours
and you were mine
Until I walked away
a fallen Angel
with wings clipped
and a halo in my pocket
No more than a human
in blue jeans
with tears in his eyes

# The stars taunt me
# littering the cosmos with their presence

It's hard to speak
of what I feel
When my vocabulary
is not set up
to speak such things
There is still a part of me
that still believes
I will see you again
and if tomorrow doesn't come
Well, I thought I saw you
the other day
but it was only a mere whisper
from my memory
The lyrics to the song
I haven't written yet
sit gentle in my mind
and I understand
there are things
I shall never finish
in this lifetime
Sometimes I need the music
and other times
the music needs me
We're not that far apart
you and I
that we can't both see the
same moon and stars
Perhaps, I didn't realize
what love truly is
until I truly learned
exactly what it isn't

# Deep in a summer red berry wine night

I've come to the conclusion
in no time
your time can be over
and perhaps I should be paying
more attention to the time that is
and not so much as it was
The truth is
You're the only one
who ever made me feel the storm
Before you, I only felt
the rain
Tonight, I'm sitting here
listening to the darkness
explain away
Why I would never understand
or come back from this
or why
I wish not to leave a shallow impression
of myself on this world
as I believe
it would be a waste of a life
Whatever is still left of me
is still waiting for the sun to come up
before I drown in my feelings
for yet another day
and it's true
tears are just words
waiting to be written down
for all to read

# It was all we knew

How many of you have cleaned an old drawer containing your grandparents old photographs? This is a true story of my own grandparents after both had passed away. I sorted through the old black and white photographs that were never put into a family album..This one particular photograph caught my attention and my imagination tried to fill in the blanks

Once I had a name
Now I'm relegated to an old image
on an old black and white photograph
yellowed by time
No one ever penned out names
or dates on the back
We are strangers to the future
long after we existed
Though the words are missing
the image projects a time
when life seemed
a lot harder than today
but we were happy
We are combat soldiers
veterans, brothers in arms
and the end is only moments away
for a few
as we fought in trenches
ankle deep in mud
in a foreign land
Once we lived
and some of us bled
and we learned how to spell
brotherly love with our blood and yet no one remembers
who we are
or the price we paid
and there is no one left to ask
if it was all worth it
It was all we knew

and no one remembers

# In this abandoned place
### (I wonder who left and never returned)

No one knows
how happy I was
to be able to feel anything
at all
The war had drained
most of my feelings out of me
Dark dreams and thoughts
permeated every waking moment
and life was reduced
to just staying alive
for as long as possible
All the while wondering
from moment to moment
would I be the next one
and would I ever see the streets
of home again
and tell Mom
today I almost died
or I'm the only one
who survived
or my best friend
was killed in action

It was all destroyed
by the reception of those
who called me a baby killer
and worse
How could I have ever
dreamed of this homecoming

Coming up on fifty
years later
I have again
picked up pen
and I'm still
afraid of the words
that might bleed out

# There are parts of you in everything I do today

I cannot be who I used to be
It's a little late for that now
and I wouldn't expect that
you could ever still be
who you used to be
but I believe I can still find
you in your own heart
I couldn't promise
the forever I wanted to
even though I would have
given you the world
What good would it have done
If I couldn't promise you
all my tomorrows as well
My unspoken words spoke louder
than the I love yous
stuck in the back of
my throat
And some names like yours
will always taste sweeter
every time I speak them
Time doesn't matter
Days turned into weeks
Weeks into months
Months into years
and years into memories
and my fingers
cannot hold onto forever
as forever is only a word

## You are every conversation
## I've ever had with my pen

I would rather live a rough life
and be passionate in what I believe, love and do
Sometimes there are silent moments
in the middle of a noise filled day
that I find myself lost
in the depth of you
Sure the moon still haunts me
when I see it hanging there
I imagine that it might do the same to you
Some days there just isn't a safe place
for a wild heart like mine to hide
and my past can't hurt me anymore
unless I let it
and It's getting harder to write poems
from my imagination
Sometimes I feel like a stranger
not knowing where to begin or end
and who can you trust with
a handful of moments
that tick away on a clock
It's been a long time since I have heard her
whisper in lower case letters in my ear
though I can still hear them echo from time to time
It was in a time when
we were the young fruit
that we carelessly consumed

# Small town

I live in a little town west of Boston
and a little north of the Pike
I was born and raised here
in a small town
We raise our kids here
living in a small white house
In a small green yard
On a tree lined paved road
With blue sky and white clouds
Where the sun always rises
and the birds always sing
in our small neighborhood
growing old
and loving you
In our small town

## Heartbreak by any other name
## would be a lie

It's funny
I don't remember
who I was
before I fell
in love with you
and now
after leaving you
I'm not sure who
I am today
and I'm wondering
who I will be
tomorrow
without you

## If he knows that he's not worth it, he will do everything so you will be saved

I always feared the forgetting
It's been a thorn of sorts
in my heart
I've tried to push away
growing older
but my body parts
are starting to fail
and my mind
with all my memories
is starting to abandon me
I suppose it's why
I chose to start here
so I won't forget
the beginning
and the end of everything
It's everything in the middle
that I'm having trouble with
these days
Some days it's harder
to lift my spirits
than it is  to carry the world
on my shoulders
and I still come with a bad name
and you're still the gold
I can't afford

# The way I see it

We've all heard it said that the past is gone
for the life, love and the lies of hope
The thirst you put in me
you aren't here to quench
you don't understand my passion for writing now
because you don't feel it
This is this, and that was that, and that is how it is
in my mind
in yours it's something else
My drink no longer holds anything of substance
that will reflect light to create rainbows
or splash in the joy during movement
Maybe it's the way the world and I
look at things now
that has turned something ugly into something beautiful
My wine glass which looks like a bunch of purple grapes
to you is not what I see, what I see is
crushed into the liquid, of poetry in motion
the taste of life, love and eternal hope

# Thanks Eddie Poe

What's that rap tap tapping at my back door
who is it I ask rather loudly
No answer is forthcoming
More rap tap tapping from my back door
I get up from my easy chair
thinking it's just the wind and nothing more
louder now the rap tap tapping from my back door
Who is it and what do you want
The voice said from the other side of the door
"I'm delivering your cookies"
Quote the girl scout, "and nothing more"

# It can't be the last time

The last time I felt like this
I saw you at an Ice cream parlor
I had to leave before I cried
The last time I felt like this
I was being shot at
by a shadowy image in the foliage
who was trying to kill me
The last time I felt like this
I wrote my poetry to ease the pain
never meaning for it to ever be read
The last time I felt like this
It was never about you
it was always about me
I am to blame for what I have done
The last time I felt like this
Even in the heat of battle
it was always about me
I couldn't let myself die
I had to make it home
The last time I felt like this
we went to the prom
I held you in my arms
and we danced the night away
The last time I felt like this
was our first kiss
The last time I felt like this
was the last time I felt like this
and I suppose it will be the last time
as time is running out
and I feel like this is
the last time

# It still hurts

I never meant to love you
But I did
and did so till it hurt
I wish I had told you that
and just like then
my words today are stuck
somewhere in my pen
waiting for the right
sheet of paper to come along
It's hard to talk
about yesterday
when it's today
so many years later

# The pedestrian under the traffic light

And if I told you I was the guy
waiting at the traffic light
for the pedestrian walk light
to change
Just so I could tell my side of the story
Would you believe me
I've been waiting a long time
for the light to change
and now
and now, I only have mere seconds
to speak my piece
before the light changes
or flashes out of order

# Rational thinking

I thought I understood
but there is always a moment of doubt
Doubt over the centuries
has reduced kingdoms
to states and countries such as ours
and doubt works against
even the lowliest of mortal humans
such as myself

There are the exit wounds
from yesterday's verbal gun fire
that bleed from time to time
My memory brings back to life
a time to challenge the doubt
before it becomes the voice
of someone else's religion
that they believe I should follow

The distance between here and there
is of no consequence to me
and I doubt the distance
is actually the truth
and it would appear to be
just another case of the
right hand not knowing
what the left hand is doing
then doubting which one
was right
before they cut off both
to solve the problem

# Something left over from yesterday

In the beginning I was born
And in the end I was formed
into what I have become
The voice inside my head
accompanies me
and it's almost too loud
When things don't add up
it's because truth
was not part of the equation
and just so you know
In the space between you and me
there never was her
or anyone else

Whenever I think of you
I almost wish we'd never met
We could be strangers instead
After all wouldn't it be better if
we didn't know each other
You'd be some woman
I wouldn't fall in love with
You know for a second
I almost believed myself

I guess I'm one of those people
that has to have the lights
left on permanently
I couldn't even say goodbye
I couldn't get it to cross my lips
My darkness consumes
the vulnerable
and I realized too late
that I was wrong
and wanted the simplest of things
to have you
look at me like we just met
and hold my hand
I was so lost

# So many words left unsaid

I know what it takes to move the pen
and I carry my excess baggage in a valise
from place to place, looking for another sheet of paper
to address the thoughts that roam in my head

When I look into your mirror
and see beauty
I realize then you need a new mirror
cause one of us is lying

The truth is hard to find
and even harder to believe in
I linger within possibilities and the diminishing worlds
of burnt out aspirations and eternal anxiety

I am a constant dancer between the words
that needs you to touch me with your eyes
and then let silence claim me as its child
Never to be found, and forever lost

# Don't forget starting tomorrow I might not be

I have moved from between
the lost and the damned
during the war
and found myself living
on borrowed dreams
and stolen love
They were my only salvation
that kept a runaway life
in focus and in check
I've always known
I would find comfort
in being who I believed
I am
not who they let me
think I have become
There just isn't a language
to express what I feel
or a sigh that can
fill the emptiness
I believe this is
where dreams end
and real life begins
and one has to be more aware
when the dead start
knocking at the door
wanting you
to come out and play
I have lived in a
comfortable delusion
and have not known
the cruel truth
until now

# Still my greatest weakness

Writing poems
counteracts my thoughts
and memories of her
Poems are only temporary
She is not

# I'm trying to find the light

Have you ever noticed
the sunshine only kisses
one side of you
first thing in the morning
and time slips away
like stars fading slowly
into the dawn
and you cannot outrun
what is meant for you
be it good or bad
By reason of my birth
I am just a regular person
among many
far from my home
but close to my house
If we never meet again
I hope I left you with more
than me touching your heart
and a question
you have to think to answer
or maybe a new thought
on your mind
and If we never meet again
I won't be able to ask for
one more
kiss
one more
hug
one more
moment
one more
touch
one more
and then another

# Here Comes tomorrow

Some nights
I lay awake
thinking about you
and wonder
if you're sleepless too
The moon found you
How come I can't

# Memories are worse than bullets

"I'm aware of my demons
I know how to control them
sometimes they escape anyway"
Ron Whittle 2016


Picking up the pieces of my life
holding them close to my nose
I inhale the smell of memories
And I wonder how could my heart
ever let me dance
with the thought of being with you
If I knew we could never be

People come and go
Many will pass through our lives
yet only a few will stand the test of time
and stand by you forever
I cannot buy love for the soul
at the market
of someone else's pleasure
and
destiny can be so uncaring

I was never entitled to you
You should have been
just out of my reach
But it was already over
once you smiled at me

Didn't anyone ever tell you
you can't cage wild things
without repercussion

# Should I ever smile at you

Should I ever smile at you
it should come with a warning
Danger thin ice
or more appropriately
warning owner consistently
says the wrong things
at inappropriate times
My lips refuse to filter out
the voice of pain
Sometimes I feel like
I'm one breath short of existence
and I don't know anymore
do I remember us
how we weren't
I guess I've been good
with my hands
and bad with my heart
and nothing will stay with us
for as long as everything still hurts
but the memories will linger on forever

# Heaven's darkness once knew the joy of the Angels

Everyday is a trial of sorts
and the only judge in life
is yourself
never pass judgement
on others before passing
sentence on oneself
Just as time knows no length
and love knows no bounds
There are shadows
deeper than the night's darkness
and love brighter than
a summer day
In another moment
life might have chosen
a different road to take
but madness and fear
took the driver's seat
and I lost half of me
and that half was you

# Three Iron nails

Inching up to the edge of my existence
words echo in the halls of time
the verse is timeless and borderless
I am not my own gospel
I am only a witness
He is the psalms of life

And the death of the truth
Is only three Iron nails away from heaven

# There is no give up here

Sutured wounds
Dead stacked like cord wood
Helicopters hover
Corpsmen run from body to body
machine guns fire
RPGs explode
Bandaged arms and legs
of men put back in the line of fire
there is no quit here
Heroes are made
the dead forgotten
Blood that was given
lives that were taken
Automatic weapons fire into the night
tracers bounce and sing
flares light the darkness
Enemy sighted
and gunned down
Mortars rain down hell on earth
death surrounds us
we never give in
and what's the cause
Pull back the perimeters
then stand your ground
there is no give up here
by the first morning light
the only thing left was those of us
who could be counted
and a surrealistic pock marked moonscape
of foliage stripped trees
and the enemy dead
Everything was burned
smoldering, blown up or destroyed
No birds no animals no grass
only dirt
The smell of cordite
and death that hung in the air

Our wounded medevaced
our dead sent home for burial
Mothers and Wives cried
and our young lives
forever altered
never to be the same

# Blue eyes in the living room

I have an urgent need
to nourish my blue eyes
once again
with her loveliness

Once
her warmth
covered me with love
and melted us into one
Alone in the room
Alone in my arms
Covered with kisses
I did not realize
how gray my existence was
until her love
colored my world

# Rain is life's chance to be touched

My early morning beach walks
are delicately balanced
between beauty and nature
I return to the ocean often
to be recharged, soothed and healed
and to have my senses
put back in order
Recently, I have come to learn
you don't just catch
someone like her
If you're lucky
like I was
to know and love her
you will also learn
like I did
It's because she let me

## What's left of old scars
## and the repeated steps of a dance that broke my feet

You are the dream
I had hoped
never to meet
I dreamt of you
who I thought
was everything
I saw you where-
ever I looked
even in the theaters
If only movies
could be real
We could have been
lovers forever

# The reality of any given moment

I don't know what it is
but I know you've got it
I can't ever quite
read your mind
I couldn't then
and I can't now
but I have this sense
that you feel
much like I do
Don't ask me to prove it
because I can't
It's only a feeling
and I don't know
how to act on it
There is no time
and
Whatever time
there was
has come and gone
but maybe just
maybe, there is
a place in forever
where we can
try and figure
it all out

# A eulogy to love

It Transcends all languages
Death and passing
Mourners mourn the dead ones
with tears
with words from a eulogy
From an epitaph carved in a stone
Do we not mourn the loss of love
in much the same way
with the tears that are cried
with the feelings of great loss
with an epitaph carved in a memory
and yet      life goes on
The memories become
like an unending eulogy
that tears at the heartstrings
and kisses the ears of those that listen
all the while silent tears well and fall
even years later
as the volume of the eulogy softly fades
with great loss

# A conduit for word play

I take issue
with anyone who
calls themselves a poet
without paper or pen
Like a bolt of lightning
inspiration
can and will strike anywhere
at any time
Being a lightning rod
a conduit for word play
the gifted are prepared
ready for the direct hit
fearing the loss of
found words
the million watt word play
finds itself on paper
rather than forever lost to the void
between the ears

# That way

I read some place once that
as we get older there's not much more
we have to learn the hard way
I accept that as the truth
I very seldom look over my shoulder anymore

Much of my life was the hard way
or the harder way
I could never find the middle of the road
or the easy way
Whatever way
always took me to the wrong way

and some day
I'm sure
I will just go the other way
or find out which way
but sooner or later it will fade away
hopefully before they come
to take me away

**Hiding secrets like sinful temptations**

Of course it was beautiful
but I'll never see it again
and I'm no better from a distance
I'm still me
One day I will realize
that we were just not meant to be

# Hope's never ending journey

There is no death to love
There is only separation
of time and space
Space can be conquered
Time however can never be brought back
or crossed over
There is only today
and maybe a tomorrow
if I'm really lucky
Yesterday is a collection of old memories
where my thoughts have resided
for so many years
It's where I have tried to make sense
of my unraveled feelings
I've been more than half way around the world
and somehow managed to survive a war
with only minor injuries
Every inch of that journey though
there was a thought about you
I never gave up hope
Hope is what kept me alive
and gave me reason to carry on living
in a time when it would have been
so easy to give up and die
It's been so many years since then
hope was put away on a closet shelf somewhere
and every now and again
I'd pull out hope
and shed a tear or two
before I put you back
I took hope down this morning
and realized how lucky I really was
to have known your love
in a time    when
that's all that mattered

# Homebody

I guess I really am a
homebody in a strange town
full of strange people
doing strange things
Why is it
when you're all alone
sadness always sets in
Perhaps the need for
a couple of shots of happiness
would do the trick
to break the ugliness
When everything is so unclear
when you're all alone
in a great big town
on a planet where no one cares
who you really are

# How do you distinguish tears from raindrops

Every night I am lulled to sleep by a false narrative
and the thoughts of a young man.
I wake wondering what words will be on my lips
when I slip into the next life
and if anyone will hear them
Then I surrender myself to the world of dreams
then wake again wondering if dreams aren't heaven
and if they are, will I dream only good things
or have the nightmares of hell for eternity
I don't want to see that moment coming
I just want to take that step in my sleep
with no regrets and no looking over my shoulder
and how do I silence the rain until then
when the tears start to fall
and there is no waking life
when it no longer wants to be woken
or when there is nothing left in life to hear
when it doesn't want to be heard
Death knows no bounds
and has no rules
It may come at anytime to anybody
and I live on pretending
that it is not so
invincible to the end
Whenever that may be

# How do you share unspoken intimacy

You know sometimes you don't realize
all the weight you've been carrying around
is just talk
Until someone comes along and listens
I sincerely think that there are too many things
left unsaid in this world
and we never fully gain the closure
that we desperately desire
and am I hanging onto something for too long
just because I think it is beautiful
Everything I do is a self portrait
and everything I write is a diary of sorts
but the words may part us
in the ending of the conversation of the heart
they like scars only fade

# If only in my mind

At the end of my childhood
when manhood was evident
and war was a definite
I dreamt about a time
that could never be
I had conversations with you
though you never knew it
And I wrote so much about you
that my fingers bled
I never intended for you to read them
but now I hope you do
Life was so very hard in those days
I don't like remembering
the bad things
only the things that kept me alive
you were the biggest part of that
you held it together for me
if only in my mind
Today light years away from yesterday
I guess you would call me arcadian
Just a simple man
with dreams
Do you remember
where it all began
I'd like to    but that memory is gone
If you still have it in your heart
share it with me please
I'm not sure who is
responsible for things I don't understand
or words
the meaning of which I cannot conceive
and when should one put the past behind them
It's hard
when many of my pleasures
in this life    are only memories
Some of which I can never let go of

# That figures

It's all that I have
All that I ever wanted
except one thing
I've already been
all that I thought
I could be
At one time
I was feeling my age
and ready for what
comes next
Now I find
there is more
before the final call
to the curtain
and now that
I'm not ready
I suppose
it's gonna come
calling on me

## If there were things I could say to you

There I was
written in poetry
Words printed on paper
on page five of the book
It's the only place you might find
traces of me
The page has been ripped out
rolled up and thrown away
It was a broken story
but taped back in place
with wrinkles and folds
as if to say
I'm sorry

# If you could only understand

You always were the stars
in my midnight sky
The celestial journey you took me on
was nothing less than pure ecstasy
But somehow I must find me
and I cry when I realize
I have to lose you
in order to do that
My head and heart do not agree
The latter destroyed me
the former killed me
I used to have it all
I just couldn't have you
no matter how much I wanted to
I will be who I am
no matter how hard
I try not to be
The dreams I built in those moments
are crushed by their own weight
and an unsaid goodbye
that I wish I could take back

# A work in progress

A work in progress
that's what I am
and have been since
the day I was born
I'm evolving
I'm not always sure
into what
I think maybe
the season of life
has clicked over
and I'm only
realizing it now
Fall is here
and Winter
is coming on
Progress is slowing
the hard way
is already completed
Cautiously
I meet the future
and
whatever is left
to do the easy way

# After all these years

I loved you and I'm sorry
seems to run together
in the same sentence
for me
I'm sorry I loved you
I loved you and I'm sorry
I treated you the way I did
I'm sorry I loved you
and never told you
I loved you
and I'm sorry
I hurt you
There, I said it
the only way
I know how
I loved you
I know it's too late

I'm so sorry

# A warm embrace of dreams

I am within you
and you in me
because of love
memories cannot be erased
and just like in the movies
in real life
we are the main characters
always just missing
connection
I never wanted you
to become the words
in someone's poetry
and here I am
writing
you and she
and yours
and how awful
I feel

# A tale of two nouns

Stop using Pro nouns
try using Amateur nouns instead
they don't command quite as much money
and they are not so hard to live with

# A story to tell

For the first time in my life
I took a look around   and realized
that   everybody has a story to tell
Some have large exciting stories
about a life filled with adventure
most, like me have short but amusing stories
about lives well lived
on a less traveled road
I cannot chronicle the stories of others
mine   seems to keep getting in the way
I stumble and fall on memories
of times I wish I could forget
The smell of burnt flesh
after all these years
is still fresh in my mind
though it's odd
and how these meet
I will never understand
during the worst times of my life
how love kept me alive
Nights when I was sickened by what I had done
to the point of being paralyzed with fear
a calm would come over me
When I would think about you
I could finally sleep knowing
that   you would be in my dreams


and you would make the mornings better

# A story behind every scar

There is a story behind every scar I bear
and for every feeling I have ever felt
Some I wish I could forget
and some long gone from memories
that time stole away
some were very good
others as bad as it can get
and then there are the ones
about the human elements
of love and death
and the struggle to stay alive
or to keep the love experience
from fading into no more than a dream
Scars have a lasting impact
on the psyche
Scars are the way the body
protects the unseen wounds
and the way I remember
your love that was lost
and those lives that I took in the war

# A silent hitchhiker to the very next page

A poet's words
should never be taken
out of context
for the wealth of the meaning
completely changes
I hate missing you
now and again
and, all the time in between
and, sometimes is never enough
Even though it's another
rainy thursday
my heart doesn't
know a thing about deadlines
nor does it care
It only recognizes
life's pains
and I'm trying to figure out
what fairytales don't tell you
There is nothing holy left in my soul
and I can't remember
if there ever was
and here I am
caught on a ride, to December again
enhancing hurt's chances
to murder me this time around

# A poet's sense

It's an art
of knowing when good
is good enough
and not going overboard
with changes
or painting over
a picture of words

# A name no one remembers

The beaten and the damned follow me into the darkness
There's something painfully familiar about this
and the silence is a stinging sound
The sound of expectations and insecurities
of the past and present

I spend my nights waiting for secrets to come
and it's only chatter and stories
I've heard hundreds of times before
Forgotten is my fate
I'm just another guy
with a name no one remembers
and I think of you sometimes
where the road meets the darkness

You're shapeless as eternity
and fleeting as a shadow
You're fearsome and you are the essence of my past
Obscured are the secrets that run rampant
in dark alleyways of my mind
and in the dank hallways of tenement buildings in dreams
And the truth is hidden beneath my bed
and like nighttime monsters
that come out to get me while I sleep

I taught you how to bleed
and never look back
Whatever you do don't ever look back
for everything is stained with metaphors
and half truths
What was once familiar
is now alien
as I meander
among the elders looking for answers
to questions yet to be asked

# The notes

A symphony of notes hanging on my clothesline
hung out to dry look like a musical poem
stretched out across the sky
I wish I knew how to read them
so I could see what they say
and I wish I could play them
to hear what they say
it always seems so complicated
when you cannot read the notes
or hear the symphony of life

# Lennon

The night it all ended
he took him from me
and you,    and us and them
never to hear his voice again
So when is a man a man
when he stands up to be counted
or lead the way
when no one else could see
We loved him so
He gave us a light to rally around
and though his words weren't very loud
everyone heard
what he had to say

all he was saying
is give peace a chance
all he was saying
is give peace a chance

# The symphony

You are the Symphony
that plays in my head
the song without words
that moves me to write
If you danced with the moon
would you still hold my hand
If I gave you my name
would you hold it in your heart
If all the stars went out
would you still make love to me
It's all too simple
anything that matters
revolves around you
My love
My life
My everything

# The sanatorium for the mind

The forest in my mind
gets progressively darker
the deeper I go in
Words hang like clouds
as thoughts fly on by
like birds in flight
much of which
I do not understand
Dreams linger
in the foliage
and overgrowth
Reality becomes
less of a tangible thing
and scary things hide
in the dark corners
of time
Memories lead me to
the paths of truth
where escape is uncertain
and may not lead
to the other side
Having no choice
I follow in the darkness
for whatever is out there
is mine
and I shall claim it
before I die

# The soles of worn out boots

My soul and spirit are worn from war
and have never completely recovered
from the wounds of the mind, sight and sound
Forgive me, if I sound trite
for that is not intended
Only the reality of the effects
of being thrown into situations
where it is impossible not to have killed
to protect our human survival instincts
I would like to be able to say
I have come home
but a very large piece of me still lays in the open battlefield
with many of my comrades in arms
And will only come home upon my passing
Much of my life today is in retrospect
reliving events I have wished to forget
Some days, I disappear into the words of others
and won't come back until I'm ready to reappear
completely absorbed in the literary refrain
of a master wordsmith
Life's puzzles loom as they linger mesmerizing
Once I was a flower
Now, I'm just another dead leaf
fodder and compost for the future to feed on
I'm just a soul who lost a love
and there are a thousand reasons
why my heart must be one with hell
Back when we were younger
but felt so much older
you were the only thing that made sense
I don't know, maybe life is too much today
Too many thoughts and impulses
crashing into one another
These words perhaps should never leave my mouth
but no matter how much I dream about
being in love, you are still gone
Like some kind of esoteric secret
I need to stop feeling like our last goodbye

was really goodbye
It's the next goodbye that really scares me

# Casting Shadows

We are only footprints
in the memory of time
and time is all consuming
that's why I don't wear a watch
and I don't believe in what mirrors say
I refuse to be that old
It's one of my many faults
I don't want pointed out
When I look back
I see the path
that got me here
it's never where I want to be
and I don't understand
why everything has to be so dirty
I'm just being realistic
about the light
that casts shadows
on the wall of my mind
and I fear
I am as lost as I have ever been
among the stars we call heaven

# Bridges to memories

There is always a before the after
I would suppose in life
there are many questions
we will never know the answers to
Who are these genius people
who understand living
It was always a game to me
Now living scares the hell out of me
actually it's the suddenness of after
and Monday mornings have never been
what I thought they would be
I am bound by my own limitations
and fears of what's over the horizon
My pen writes words that once lived before
to you the reader they're just words
to me they are bridges to memories
that I wish to have live on
After

# Broken rules

I've always been in favor of
breaking all the rules
Rules are meant to be broken
Laws are meant to be followed
Rule breakers are natural born leaders
that know how to get around
and skirt the big issues
for those that do not matter
in the over all scheme of things
Rule breakers are not cheaters
they've just found a shorter way
to get to point B
or found a better answer
for the age old questions
In my mind
any formula that shortens a mathematical
rhetorical question is a good one
Explanations are not always necessary
methods normally are

# Better half

I've heard it said
that you're my better half
I want to know if that's true
then which is my worst half
the top half or the bottom half
or is it my left side or my right
And why didn't they say
you're my very best half
Someone didn't give you enough credit

# At my back door

At my back door
knocks the verse
I was looking for.
The dog barks
as I let it in
Quickly it finds
the prose I write
and settles in on
the final line
Words that live
where I play
and live on for
eternity
I only borrow
and do not steal
for they are not
mine to keep
only to use
to fill the void
in the chorus
in my mind

# An empty shell 1969

I feel so different
like I had no heart or soul left
Just an empty shell of a man
wandering from one to another
meaningless relationships
I could never find what I gave up
surrounded by the darkness
overwhelmed with pain
no one feels the loneliness
when no one hears you cry

# Always isn't forever

For always
isn't forever
so why would you say that
Is it me just being overly sensitive
I gave myself forever not for always
I thought you did too
for always isn't enough
I need more
I want all of you
not just the parts you wanted to give
or parts you wanted to take back
there are shadows being cast
in multiple directions
which one is yours

# Along the path of life

I know I'm a crazed old dude
wrapped up in a sixty eight year old frame
but I am still relevant
and have learned much along the path of life
wisdom learned from my own mistakes
and fighting back the demons
lesson one
Love the way you live
and live the way you love
everything after that is secondary
and really doesn't matter

# The tide of dreams

I ride the tide of dreams
alone in the water that surrounds me
drifting with the seaweed
glancing toward the shore
I swim against the surging sea
my job is to rescue you
from my morning dreams
that spin tales of those things
that never will be
reaching out to yet another day
I shall dream of you again
and set out to rescue
the floundering truth
from near certain death
in the depths of the sea

# The used book store

My words gather momentum
as they seemingly run downhill
Occasionally picking up a sentence or two
or maybe even a phrase
These are the thoughts coming from my head
I write in the belief that
sometime a hundred years from now
I will get discovered
in an out of date used book store
By someone much like myself
Someone who wonders
about the pains of a life well lived
the opening of a door
or looking out any window
and seeing a different life view
It's how I paint that scene with words
so all can understand
and to see what I did

## Every mouth I ever kissed, was just practice, until there was yours

I'm not too far away from
the fire
I'm not afraid to love
and my feet are not
afraid to walk away

But I am carved
by the hungry fools
who want to devour my heart
and somehow I became
my own worst enemy
Loss seems inevitable
as I have seen the exit signs
and I need to stop
ending sentences
with goodbye

I'm tired of the plastic
compassion of others
who consider themselves
well adjusted
I want to stop apologizing
for the actions of the neurotic
with the sterilized smiles
and stainless steel edges

We are all struggling to survive
in a broken world where we
remember old photographs
of long gone parents
and loves that came
and just as suddenly left
and I don't want to waste words
on I told you so
and I wish I had
When I just didn't listen to
the words don't go

# This is the way it was

I wanted to tell you
I was not certain what I felt
I wanted you
but I was so frightened
by the want
These words tomorrow might not
carry the meaning they have tonight
I want to believe
I was myself
but the truth is
I was only
what you thought I was
and tomorrow
holds no more promise
than today did
I overflow with words
but they don't fill
the emptiness
and I'm sorry
you got the version
of me that I wasn't
All I ever wanted
was to sleep with
your dreams
and hold you in
my arms

# Gone is the melody that played in my head

I just want you to know I never kissed you
with another's name on my lips
I just want you to know
there never was anyone else
I loved you too much to do that
I just want you to know
you were everything I ever wanted
I just want you to know
The stars swung back and forth
and spun as if on a string
and the moon has no reason to come out
to do the same thing
I just wanted you to know

Really,

I just want you to know

# No refuge

There is no refuge from my words
that haunt my mind
and even when I'm Whiskey blind
I can still speak the truth
When I write my poems
the words are like a Carpenter who carries tools
but asks not what to build
and from whatever madness comes from the moon
it speaks thru my pen
to the pad of paper on my desk
My thoughts are like leaving a book open
to the wind that changes pages
with each blowing breeze
Some days I long for silence in my brain
and when I do get that silence
I get frightened that I have lost the words
and I wonder if the silence will last forever
and I wonder when and if
that day will ever come

# The sun shines through the wind

And here I am
perfect strangers with someone else
all over again
not knowing what to expect
not knowing what to do
and if I don't breathe
it doesn't hurt anymore
okay, so I'm not perfect
I am messy and have secrets
and I'm barely housebroken

# So what's your name

So let me ask you this
Can a star be bought
or traded or even gifted to you
Will your wish ever come true
Does stardust really fall from the sky
Are we really made from carbon
expelled from a star implosion
from a million billion years ago
If that's true what was your star's name
and why aren't you named that today
Where in the night sky did you come from
Will you ever go back
and would you take me with you
and if you do I will give to you
the purest form of earth bound carbon
to wear on your finger
So you can sparkle once again
in the midnight sky

## Maybe it's too romantic
## but something about the truth
## always makes me smile

If I found myself in a room full
of things I lost in my lifetime
it wouldn't take long
to realize you were the most
important one
I am not what happened to me
I am what I chose to become
I gave you up, so you could have
what I could not give you
Love is not always about
lies and cheating
Sometimes, it's just for the best
This may have been
too much love for one lifetime
and sadly, I will miss
what I missed
forever

## The mountains we can not see
## until we open our eyes

Reality will always mimic another day
while the Sun reaches its highest zenith
to try and seduce the blue of the sky
A bright contrast to the cloudiness
the war has left me with
as damaged goods
I am vulnerable to bouts of depression
and it's all relative and temporary
cause when I die no one will remember
but my poetry will always know my pain
And everything still inches forward
in the renaissance of daybreak
as I strive to live within my inner peace
but forever and ever
is well beyond my ability to grasp
and the ideals of love and promised gems
that hasn't blossomed even in the warmth
of the new light of another summer day
Here, there, now, nowhere
In this, the timeless dance
the warrior hangs like
an albatross around my neck
begging to be set free

## It's my life you can have it if you want it

I go from bad to worse
and back again
Me and my oil paints and brushes
making a statement piece
for the world to see
I have a whole studio
full of one piece
Hung on my wall
I see it      I paint it
I hear it      I write it
I speak it      I get sued for plagiarism

So much for my signature piece
I can never seem to win

## Because what happens right now, in this moment is only temporary

Life is always looking for a
better version of something
and it's nothing we can return
to the sender
Life is only available
for a limited amount of time
and we learn early on
that if it's right it happens,
nothing good gets away
The past hasn't changed
but we have
Life goes on
and builds momentum
at a downhill speed
and holding hands we face
the rising tide and wander
off into the undertow of life
Just as some of the stars
can only exist
when we turn off the lights

# Stolen breaths

Specks of starlight grow in her eyes
and stolen breaths rest on untouchable flesh
So he decided, she was not a new chapter in his book
She is the entire book
She was the lace on his leather
and he knew he'd never breathe her words again
or smell the scent of her skin
He stands at both ends of the unknown
Lost to his true self
and lost to her love
They were tragically beautiful
The night calls and they listen
the voices come and whisper things
they choose to ignore
They both refuse to acknowledge the truth
and keep living as if this night
was a lifetime

# Escaping the reach of the shadows

Even though
we didn't need a name for it
we both knew what it was
God, even the vowels in her name
got excited when someone
called out her name
I have missed her
so much

# Tales of a veteran of war

Even though
it might have looked like it
I was not
looking to change
the world
one bullet at a time
I was trying
to save my piece of it

# Promises

I try to keep the promises I make
sometimes it's just impossible
I don't like making promises
Promises by their nature are hard to keep

I don't know why
but it always seems
I'm writing on scraps of paper
when a whole sheet cannot be found
Such is the story of my life
just like making my promises

Even in the darkness of night
you are the guiding light
the lamp that lights my way
Who understands
when the promises I make
are like the sheet of paper
that cannot be found

# The second amendment bandage

If she hadn't smiled
I'd have never known
the likes of a loaded gun
She could get me so weak
I'd forget the language
her bullets speak in

# Under the influence of a controlled substance

Okay so I was
under the influence
of Lawrence Ferlinghetti
R D Laing, Allen Ginsburg
and a few other nonconformists
Socially drunk with admiration
that left me slightly disabled
and a little blind
I followed in the footsteps
of these literary giants
on a voyage of discovery
and was swallowed
by the vision of the future
through the eyes
of these prodigious thinkers
The magic transformation
of my world centered me
way to the right of life.
Intoxicated with the uncontrolled
substance of composition and discourse
At times I would fumble with the words
or lack the ability to express myself
with feeling from deep within
or to be real and honest
but I can't
I come up empty and frightened
as my pen runs dry of ink
and learned that
expressionism is a form
of self imprisonment
from which break out is impossible
and when was it that
real became wrong
and honesty became so complex

# Heaven once gave me one of it's angels

Ripped from the darkest corners
of crumpled pages
Torn from my manuscript
I write
words that read
I was not her ghost
but she was mine

# Miserably right

I'd rather laugh than be
miserably right all the time
I admit it
I can be as wrong as the next guy
sometimes even wronger
if there is such a word
I tried it once,  being right all the time
I didn't like it
I'd rather be human and make mistakes
and learn to live with them
Please
Forgive me when I'm wrong
and love me even more
when I'm right

# I can feel the angels watching us,
## shaking their heads

It's funny I never know what
the right words are to say
except I am the judge and jury
of my own self interests
Something old must die
before something new can rise from the ashes

As my time draws to a close and nearing the end
I am acutely aware of that
In the family there will be
one coming and one going

But I take comfort in knowing
that our love still exists somewhere
Even though it's only in our names
we are still together
Right there where I carved our names
in a heart, on the birch tree
in your old front yard

I wonder if anyone ever
traces their finger around the heart
and wonders who we are

## Growing loud and tall until I heard your name

How can it get any louder
than this
I was told I was
an original
A one of a kind
A renaissance man
A man among men
I laugh
I am only me
who plays with words
and sometimes in the sandbox

# A one way ticket to perception

Words have never been enough to describe a scene
it takes color and a steady hand
and the proper use of shadows and light
Art is but an escape mechanism
defined by the colors used
and who is it that is that Artist
that can transform the surreal
into picture perfect

Art does not need anyone to
validate its existence
nor does it need anyone to criticize
the use of the medium
in the mind's eye of the Artist
Art is the expression of the exposed
soul made visible
through the astuteness of the flawed

Art is the deciphered use
of brush or knife to canvas
to freeze a moment in time
that words could never quite
breathe life into
Leaving the viewer as a traveler
with a oneway ticket to perception
to fill the space between eye, mind and taste

# It's way too late to say goodbye

In the past, I've failed with intimacy
with those words left unspoken
I was terrified that I would lose myself in you
Truthfully, I already had since day one
Did I expect my sorrys to help, no
and they won't fix the cracks in your heart
and I know the heartbreak will always
be signed with my name on it
Yet, I still toy around with my thoughts
like a lost puppy trying to find his home
hoping somebody has left the door open
I'm sorry
I couldn't be the kind of better
that you so rightfully deserved
and I'm sorry you never saw
the writing on the wall

where I wrote
I love you
at least a million times

# Credits and Acknowledgements

Thank you John Tsombakos for believing in me when no one else did ( Mister T was my Senior High School English Teacher.  He was and always will be the original Mister T.  Rest in Peace my mentor you did your job well  April 14, 2016 )

Thank you Reggie Aguis for keeping my first manuscript when I lost mine

Thank you Linda McLeod Cowart for giving me inspiration when I needed to cling onto something real and beautiful in a time of ugliness and war

Thank you Kathi Keddy Giotta for everything you have done for me. Without you none of this would have been possible.  All the late night laughs, discussions and meatballs too.  But I still think I make better red gravy than you.

Thank you David Macpherson of the Hangover Hour Spoken Salon for your support and giving me the chance at my first reading.  Your encouragement is greatly appreciated

Thank you Nicholas Earl Davis and Alex Charalambides of the Dirty Gerund Poetry Show for your support and for allowing me to read at your shows

A special thanks to my Wife, Children, Grandchildren and other family members. I love you one and all.

Ronald J. Whittle,

a lifetime resident of Massachusetts, was born in Worcester and raised and educated in his home town of Shrewsbury. Further education came by way of the U.S. Navy, Vietnam, the Apollo 13 recovery team, and 45 years of family living. Ron divides his time between his home in Worcester and the shores of Cape Cod. His influences include Tom Waits, Lawrence Ferlinghetti, Edgar Allan Poe, Ogen Nash, Ezra Pound and Rod McKuen. Ron is a member of the Worcester County Poetry Association, the Works in Progress/ Outlaw Stage at the Worcester Artist Group, a founding member of the Worcester Art Walk, and a member of the Warrior Writers of Boston. Ron's work can be found on Amazon, eBooks, ePoetry sites and at readings throughout New England.

www.ingramcontent.com/pod-product-compliance
Lightning Source LLC
Chambersburg PA
CBHW071128090426
42736CB00012B/2057